A Quire of Paper
Maura Dooley

smith|doorstop

Published 2015 by
smith|doorstop Books
The Poetry Business
Bank Street Arts
32-40 Bank Street
Sheffield S1 2DS

ISBN 978-1-910367-41-4
Typeset by Utter
Printed by MPG Biddles

Acknowledgements
With many thanks to the staff, trustees, volunteers and visitors to
Jane Austen's home at Chawton.

smith|doorstop Books are a member of Inpress:
www.inpressbooks.co.uk. Distributed by Central Books Ltd.,
99 Wallis Road, London E9 5LN

The Poetry Business gratefully acknowledges the support
of Arts Council England.

Contents

Distribute the affectionate love of a heart
not so tired as the right hand belonging to it.

– letter to Cassandra, December 9th 1808

A Visit

I walk in, Jane,
and we sit by the fire,
outside the swallows dip and soar

rain keeps us in
this late cold spring,
mud clogs the lane, the day is raw,

we watch the swallows
shred the air with quick bright strokes,
wind shakes the door

a shiver passes through the room,
I see the flames first spark,
then roar.

Why Do We Come?

Because she says what we think, quietly,
she says what we think, wittily,
with more wit,
before we knew we thought it.

Because we read her at school, at college,
in bed alone,
we made a life teaching others about her
and we like the dresses.

Because we know about Shakespeare,
Heathcliff, Harry Potter and Jane,
and they said that a day out with a pub lunch
is an English tradition .

Because a parent said *here, you might like this one,*
and we tried it and we did.

'Objects Found Under the Floorboards'

A penknife, a spoon, a hinge, a file, a stopper,
we cannot explain the things brought up from under,

the small gun, the pipe, a doll's plate, a button,
stained or dusty, bright and brassy, forgotten,

the familiarstrange: a story we try to place,
still lives, held in wait so patiently. That face?

The Seedling

Quercus Robur, replanted in 1986 by Miss J Bowden, Curator

Who knows where a seed might fall?
An acorn's self-sown sapling coaxed
from shade beside the garden wall
found safety in this rich and fertile
ground, in this fond earth. English Oak.
Your tree, Jane. Each Spring its leaves
bunch into life, wind whispers through.

Who was that spoke?

The Subjunctive Mood

Well, we know that
she may have
she might have
she probably would have
they tended to
possibly
in those days.

We can assume that
evidence suggests
she is said to have
we can certainly imagine that
indeed, it is likely
at that time

and we could conclude from this
perhaps,
an informed guess
but anyway,
we have the novels.

Under the Eaves

A small cemetery of flies,
the wing of a tigermoth, an ancient bee
and here beside the Pheremoth trap,
a broken chair, dull watercolours, dust cloths,
a mannequin in narrow satin stands
by the rain-streaked window whose six
even panes frame sheep, starlings, a roof,
a sloping meadow, an elm and everchanging skies
which now and then, before and after chores,
spill moonlight into an unloved space.
Dreams will have raided this quiet place.

Capt Frank Austen Visits Port Mahon

My dear Cassandra – Frank is made. – He was yesterday raised to the rank of
Commander & appointed to the Petterel
Jane Austen: letter to her sister, Cassandra, 28th December 1798

Strangely, you're still here on this Mediterranean island
hugger-mugger at Fiesta, where a sweat of gin and sun,
the clatter and heft of steaming horses, an immaculate caixer's
rosewater blessing and even the summer holiday scent
of *Piz Buin* summons the skin-sore sailor's salve
of almond oil. So, the tang of the old port rises
condensing on a Georgian windowpane through which,
on the blue serge sea, we might glimpse a sail fill,
a sloop turn in the breeze and slip away towards Gibraltar.

> ## Milk of Roses — Capt Frank Austen's recipe
> *from Martha Lloyd's collection of recipes gathered in the*
> *Austen family's Household book*
>
> 1/2 pint of rosewater,
> 1/2 oz of oil of sweet almond,
> 12 grains salt of tartar,
> to be mixed well altogether.

A Fancy
at Chawton House

Sheep, clover, limeflowers,
bramble blousy with blossom,
                                    bees,
the burst and scatter of daisies,
a stand of elm and this birch
                            circled with ivy,
blazing with birdsong, warm wind winnowing leaves,
summer's breath,
                        and in that moment,
the switch of a muslin skirt .

'Have you Remembered to Collect Pieces for the Patchwork?'

Jane Austen: letter to her sister, Cassandra, Friday May 31ˢᵗ 1811

The mind shakes out a bolt of plain muslin

                                   which billows

then is caught, smoothed, held and pinned
before the *fussy cutting* begins:

                           the snipping and placing
of pieces to make shape, pattern and shade.

Precisley twelve stitches to the inch,
tension perfected in a line of thread,

                         in a lightning needle,
in and out, sharp and fine, gleaming as it draws it all together.

Quire of Paper

A froth heated just enough to settle and firm
or crisp lightly at the edges,
delicate,
a mixture to reward the pressure of attention
with sustenance, new flavour,
delicious,
and fine enough to let the light flood through.

Thin cream pancakes, called Quire of Paper
*from Martha Lloyd's collection of recipes gathered
in the Austen family's Household book*

Take to a pint of cream eight eggs leaving out two
whites, three spoonfuls of fine flour, three spoonfuls
of sack and one spoonful of orange flower water, a
little sugar, a grated nutmeg and a quarter pound of
butter melted in the cream. Mingle all well together,
mixing the flour with a little cream at first that it may
be smooth. Butter your pan for the first pancake, and
let them run as thin as possible to be whole. When
one side is coloured it is enough. Take them carefully
out of the pan and strew some fine sifted sugar
between each. Lay them as evenly on each other as
you can. This quantity will make twenty.

The Visitors' Book

I am finally here.
A place of pilgrimage.

I am honoured to walk where once she walked.

Her books have taught me to hope:
before, I scarcely ever allowed myself to hope.

This place, full of secrets.

Merveilleux!
Wunderschön!
Bellisimo!
Fantabadozie!

My sister, Jane.

I'm bringing my Dad.

Considering the Donkey Cart

Here is the horse and carriage of a modest household
the means of escape on muddy days, drab days,
days when to whisper into the tender ears that Midas wore,
to tickle behind the teasing ears that Bottom desported
was to know the thrill of the open gate, the bright road
stretching away.
                    Ah Jack! Ah Jenny!

Ra chose you, Jesus chose you, Sancho chose you
but who can coax your bony back, your stony look,
uncomfortable, unbiddable, mired happily, enduring,
eschewing the tasty barley, chewing a thistle, who can
tempt you to carry *the king with the golden crown*
or lift these sisters' spirits with a day in Town?

At the Grave of Cassandra and Mrs Austen

St Nicholas's Church, Chawton

Though mother and daughter
I'd thought of them as babes-in-the-wood
tucked up, snug, beneath a quilt of moss,
their lullaby the soft tattoo of owl,
the flit flit flit of bat and I'd sorrowed
for the absent sister, far from home –
the green lane, the warm kitchen, the creaking door,
all the comforts of the familiar translated
by death to brass and marble –
but now I see the grave for what it is,
a plot of stone and earth in shade,
now I picture them at work elsewhere,
their hands gathering folds of cambric,
morning-light flooding their cheerful faces.